LOOK UP

**Written by
Richard Vaughan**

D0061560

ScottForesman

A Division of HarperCollins*Publishers*

Look up in the sky
and what can you see?

A sun that gives light.

A moon that shines at night.

Stars that twinkle in the sky.

5

A comet that flashes by.

A planet that has many rings.

Space is full of many things!